TAMING THE FINGERS

TAMING THE FINGERS

Heavenly Wisdom for Social Media

Jeff Johnson
Foreword by Tim Challies

Reformation Heritage Books
Grand Rapids, Michigan

Reformation Heritage Books
3070 29th St. SE
Grand Rapids, MI 49512
616–977–0889
orders@heritagebooks.org
www.heritagebooks.org

Scripture taken from the New King James Version®. Copyright © 1982 by Thomas Nelson. Used by permission. All rights reserved.

Printed in the United States of America
23 24 25 26 27 28/10 9 8 7 6 5 4 3 2 1

Library of Congress Cataloging-in-Publication Data

Names: Johnson, Jeff W. (Pastor), author.
Title: Taming the fingers : heavenly wisdom for social media / Jeff
    Johnson ; foreword by Tim Challies.
Description: Grand Rapids, Michigan : Reformation Heritage Books, 2023.
Identifiers: LCCN 2022054860 (print) | LCCN 2022054861 (ebook) |
    ISBN 9798886860061 (paperback) | ISBN 9798886860078 (epub)
Subjects: LCSH: Oral communication—Religious aspects—Christianity. |
    Social media—Religious aspects—Christianity. | Christian life. | Bible.
    Proverbs—Criticism, interpretation, etc.
Classification: LCC BV4597.53.C64 J64 2023 (print) | LCC BV4597.53.
    C64 (ebook) | DDC 248.4—dc23/eng/20230310
LC record available at https://lccn.loc.gov/2022054860
LC ebook record available at https://lccn.loc.gov/2022054861

For additional Reformed literature, request a free book list from Reformation Heritage Books at the above regular or email address.

*This book is dedicated to the
loving memory of my father-in-law,*

Frank Chase (1955–2022),

a man who bought the truth
and did not sell it (Prov. 23:23).

CONTENTS

FOREWORD

It was not very long ago that residents of Richmond, Virginia, felt the ground beneath them begin to shake. They did what people do these days—they opened Twitter and shared the news of an earthquake. Thirty seconds later, the tremors hit New York City, and by that time, many people had already read the tweets and knew an earthquake was on its way. This was just one demonstration of the incredible power and unparalleled speed of social media.

With such a powerful medium in our pockets or in our hands at all times, we need to be absolutely certain that we are equipped to handle it well. Because whatever else we know of technology, we know this: it always brings both benefits and drawbacks. Our modern technologies allow us wonderful opportunities to express our love for God and our fellow man but also horrifying opportunities to dishonor God and harm our fellow man. That choice is before us every time we unlock our device.

Thankfully, the wisdom we need is offered to us in God's Word, the Bible. The wisdom that guided our forebears is the same wisdom that ought to guide us today. In this excellent little book, Jeff Johnson teaches us how to master modern-day challenges through words of ancient wisdom. He dives into the Proverbs to teach us that the great challenge of our day is not first one of technology but one of character. He shows that if we are to serve God's purpose through all these amazing new apps and devices, we will need to carefully and prayerfully tame our fingers.

—Tim Challies
Author of *Seasons of Sorrow*

INTRODUCTION

Sin does not operate independently from tools. It puts things into its service by the influence of the Wicked One. One of those things in the present generation is social media. I began writing this book on the heels of and in response to the events of 2020, which, in my judgment, proved this beyond the slightest doubt. COVID-19 hit us, and when it did, most of us were held up in our homes and frustrated, some of us were out of work, a good number of us were scared, and nearly all of us had strong opinions about how the pandemic should be handled by the government and by the church. Concerns resurfaced about racism and oppression. The 2020 election for United States president was a huge matter of contention. The claims of a stolen election, the storming of the capitol building in DC, and the second impeachment of Donald Trump were all unprecedented in American history. I was grieved at how professing Christians were acting angrily, sarcastically, or rudely in response to those events on social media. Those events are getting further in the rearview mirror, and things have died down to some degree. But what will the next big thing be that will spark controversy and threaten the unity of Christians?

Let me be clear. I am not against social media. I do not believe it was designed in the devil's conference room as he met with the powers of darkness. Thus, the answer is not for us to abandon social media, labeling it as evil. Instructing believers to put down the tool might only serve to feed spiritual pride, resulting in us manifesting the sins committed on social media in some other way (Col. 2:20–23). Social media can be a wonderful tool to communicate, connect with people, and share a measure of our lives with one another. However, unless we understand how to use social media wisely, we will be accessories to Satan's destructive purposes.

Speaking and Writing

This book is designed to be intensely practical. In it, I seek to apply what the book of Proverbs teaches about communication to our use of social media. Proverbs has much to say about how we use our mouths and our tongues—i.e., our words. The problem with social media is that we might not make the connection between what we say and what we write (type). Scripture, on the other hand, makes a direct connection between what one says and what one writes. God Himself is the supreme example of this. Scripture, the written Word, is what He says (Gal. 3:8; see Gen. 12:3). The apostle Paul understood what he wrote in his letters to be no different from his spoken words (Gal. 5:16). When we understand that what we write is equivalent to what we speak, then we will be careful to apply all that Scripture says concerning communication to our use of social media.

Heavenly Wisdom versus Earthly Wisdom

The apostle Paul says in 1 Corinthians 1:30 that Christ has been made unto us "wisdom from God." A large portion of that wisdom has been deposited in the book of Proverbs, which means that Proverbs is not a collection of helpful hints. It is not street smarts or mere sage advice. It is more than common sense. It is heaven-sent wisdom from Christ to give us the insight we need to live in God's world, God's way. We must constantly and consciously choose God's wisdom rather than the corrupt wisdom of this fallen world. Before we try to apply the wisdom of Proverbs to our use of social media, let's briefly consider a contrast between heavenly wisdom and earthly wisdom. The apostle James writes:

> Who is wise and understanding among you? Let him show by good conduct that his works are done in the meekness of wisdom. But if you have bitter envy and self-seeking in your hearts, do not boast and lie against the truth. This wisdom does not descend from above, but is earthly, sensual, demonic. For where envy and self-seeking exist, confusion and every evil thing are there. But the wisdom that is from above is first pure, then peaceable, gentle, willing to yield, full of mercy

and good fruits, without partiality and without
hypocrisy. Now the fruit of righteousness is sown
in peace by those who make peace. (James 3:13–18)

James makes this contrast between heavenly wisdom
and earthly wisdom immediately after admonishing
us to tame our tongues because of the tremendous
damage that this little member of our body can do
(3:1–12). This contrast between heavenly wisdom and
earthly wisdom also immediately precedes instruc-
tion concerning conflict (4:1–12). James wants us to
understand how heavenly wisdom shapes our communication in contrast to how earthly wisdom shapes
our communication.

James says earthly wisdom is envious, and its goal
is to win (that is, it is self-seeking). In contrast, heavenly wisdom is pure in its motives and genuinely seeks
peace. Earthly wisdom is arrogant and lies. It does not
necessarily communicate bald-faced lies. Instead,
it lies by not checking facts before communicating
information, or it lies by refuting something before
doing its homework. Why does earthly wisdom do
this? Remember, its main concern is to win. Because
of this goal, it always creates "confusion and every evil
thing." Earthly wisdom destroys relationships.

Heavenly wisdom is gentle. Rather than using
information as a tool to win, it is willing to yield.
The person possessed with heavenly wisdom is easily
entreated. He or she listens to reasonable arguments
and also presents reasonable arguments. Heavenly

wisdom is also full of mercy. It is not harsh and eager to judge. Heavenly wisdom is full of good fruits, which include all Christian virtues. Divine wisdom that comes from above is impartial so that it does not show favoritism. It treats everyone by the same standard. If something is right for one person, it is right for everyone. It does not condemn one act as wrong while ignoring or minimizing other acts of evil. It does not praise righteousness in one situation while ignoring it in another. Why do you think someone would be partial in his or her communication? Since the goal of earthly wisdom is to win, it condemns evil and praises virtue only as necessary to accomplish that goal. Heavenly wisdom is free of hypocrisy since it seeks peace on the basis of truth.

Only two options exist. We apply either heavenly wisdom or earthly wisdom to our use of social media. And as James teaches us, the results of this choice are drastically different. My hope is that this little tour through Proverbs will encourage us to bring forth the good fruit of heavenly wisdom.

The Fear of God

How can we attain to heavenly wisdom and avoid earthly wisdom in our communication? The answer is *the fear of God*. "The fear of the LORD is the beginning of wisdom, and the knowledge of the Holy One is understanding" (Prov. 9:10). One aspect of the fear of the Lord is living with the awesome awareness that we are *always* under His all-seeing eye (Prov. 15:3).

Nothing about us is hidden from His sight, including the secret thoughts and intentions of our hearts (Heb. 4:12). The Lord's eyes are upon us when we sit in our easy chair with the computer or in the car with our smartphone in hand. When we are ready to post on social media, He sees the motives, He sees the matter, and He sees the manner. When we live with this awesome awareness, our chief concern is to please Him in all that we do (2 Cor. 5:9), knowing that we will give an account at the judgment (2 Cor. 5:10). This includes giving an account for our words (Matt. 12:34–37). We do not consider this as an unwelcome intrusion on our lives when we are truly regenerate, because as believers, we desire His praise above all else (1 Cor. 4:5). The fear of God is foundational to heavenly wisdom because it sends us to the Scriptures to seek out what pleases Him in all aspects of life, and this includes our use of social media.

I have broken down what Proverbs says about communication by asking five questions to help us cultivate heavenly wisdom in our use of social media:

- Am I controlled?
- Am I calm?
- Am I careful?
- Am I compassionate?
- Am I conscientious?

I neither intend nor pretend this to be exhaustive, but I hope that it is enough to get us thinking in the right direction.

Chapter 1

AM I CONTROLLED?

How many times have you read or heard things like this: "You must not be silent!" "Christians need to speak out!" "Silence is violence!" The idea is that to be silent, by default, is to score a run for the other team. What is concerning about this kind of rhetoric is that it indicates how few understand the virtue and value of silence (Amos 5:13). The virtue of silence is a form of self-control, one of the fruits of the Spirit (Gal. 5:22). The Spirit enables believers to consciously and deliberately control our appetites, our thoughts, our emotions, and our *words*. Sadly, social media has revealed a tremendous lack of self-control among professing Christians. Don't misunderstand me. Silence can be sinful. But nowhere does Scripture teach that it is your duty to speak out every time there is an opportunity to do so. When you believe speaking out is your duty or you choose to do so, self-control will manifest itself by remaining silent until two things are true: your spirit is tame, and your speech is timely.

Your Spirit Is Tame

Apparently, some people think that communicating what is on their minds is a virtue. At least they're not phonies, right? You can't fault them for being honest, can you? Some, perhaps, would define this as boldness. If no one else is willing to say it, they are willing to be the lightning rod to take strikes for the truth. A more timid-natured person might find himself admiring this "virtue," wishing that he had such intestinal fortitude. But this is not a virtue. It is not Spirit-given boldness. It is a lack of self-control. Proverbs 29:11 says, "A fool vents all his feelings, but a wise man holds them back." A literal rendering from the Hebrew text does not limit this to anger. It can be translated as, "The fool always brings forth his spirit, but the wise man stills it." The basic idea is that the fool *always* lets people know *all* that is going on in his mind and heart. He holds nothing back.

So, let's say a particular issue is on your mind. You are greatly exercised over it. You want everyone to be set straight about it. So, you type out your thoughts, and you press the magic button that sends it to hundreds of people at once. Then you wait—for all of about ten seconds before checking back for responses, ready to defend the cause with ready-made or off-the-cuff arguments. Or, perhaps, someone else has posted their thoughts and perspectives. Whether you agree or disagree, you scroll past it at first. You scroll up. You scroll down. You try your best to ignore it. You leave your computer or cell phone. But you just can't take it. You've just got to put in your two cents. Is it wrong to do so? No, not necessarily. However, that inner sense of compulsion is likely *not* the fire of truth welling up in your bones that will not let you rest until you speak for the cause of righteousness (Jer. 20:9). More than likely, it is an untamed spirit at work.

The wise man holds back. "He who has knowledge spares his words, and a man of understanding is of a calm spirit" (Prov. 17:27). It is not that the wise man never reveals what he is thinking and feeling. He exercises self-control over his spirit so that he does not disclose all of his thoughts and emotions. Some of them he may never reveal. Such a person is truly strong, especially when it comes to holding back anger. "He who is slow to anger is better than the mighty, and he who rules his spirit than he who takes a city" (Prov. 16:32). The world may praise those who are not afraid to voice all their opinions. But the quietest and most hesitant to speak are usually the strongest, and those who talk the most are usually the weakest. "Whoever has no rule over his own spirit is like a city broken down, without walls" (Prov. 25:28). One reason the wise man holds back is that he understands that the more he communicates, the greater the likelihood he is going to sin. Proverbs 10:19 says, "In the multitude of words sin is not lacking, but he who restrains his lips is wise." The less you communicate, the more you cut down on the possibility of sinning.

In my opinion, social media makes it more difficult to keep your spirit under control and to restrain your lips (your fingers, in this case). This is so because social media seems to be void of many of the barriers that are present in other forms of communication. I do not know who first said it, but it is certainly true: technology giveth, and technology taketh away. The technology that has given us social media has taken away much of the quality control that governs communication. For example, when speaking in person with someone, you can pick up on signals and body language that indicate you ought not continue in that direction with the conversation. It could be as simple as a look on someone's face that makes you think, If I keep talking this way, I might get punched. While speaking with someone on the phone, you may hear sighs, or the person may get very quiet. This indicates that your words are not having the intended effect. This kind of quality control is essentially nonexistent with social media. Social media makes us braver, too. It is easy to be fearless when typing in the privacy and safety of your home or car.

Social media is also different than writing a letter. It is a different process. A letter allows much more time to think. You erase and pen different words. You crumple up the paper, throw it in the wastebasket, and start over, especially when it is regarding a sensitive subject. The fact that you have to fold up the finished product, stuff it into an envelope, address the envelope, get a stamp, and mail it gives you time to change your mind. It is nowhere near as fast as pressing Enter, Send, Post, or Share. Barriers exist. Caution lights slow us down, and red lights tell us to stop. Social media, however, allows for the immediate expression of our thoughts and quick responses. In fact, you do not even have to use words. There are symbols and emojis, which, of course, can communicate precisely all that words can convey (I am waxing sarcastic). Can you imagine receiving a letter in the mail and responding to it by sending back a drawing of a thumbs-up or a sad face? We need to consider seriously how social media is void of built-in quality control that is more conducive to facilitating the taming of our spirits. However, if you decide to use social media as a platform to communicate your thoughts and discuss issues, you should always make sure that your spirit is tame.

The most basic and foundational way to tame your spirit is to obey Proverbs 4:23, which says, "Keep your heart with all diligence, for out of it spring the issues of life." That means to guard your heart or keep watch over it as one would a prison. When guarding a prison, you are trying to keep people from escaping. To guard your heart diligently is to identify the sinful disposition that is influencing an ungodly action and prevent it from coming out. This does not mean, of course, you are to be content merely to keep it within your heart. That fosters hypocrisy. It means you are

to address the sinful disposition by confessing it to
the Lord, seeking cleansing in His blood, and putting
it to death by the Spirit before it breaks out and does
damage. In the case of an untamed spirit, I can almost
guarantee that the sinful disposition that escapes is
pride. If you are having trouble with an untamed
spirit, examine your heart, and ask yourself a couple of
questions. Ask yourself, Am I extremely irritated when
I believe so many do not hold my perspective or conviction on an issue? If the answer is yes, then pride in
the heart, unless addressed, will not allow you to rest
until you have spoken. Perhaps it is an important issue
where people need to be instructed and corrected. But
that leads to the next question. Ask yourself, What is
my motive for wanting to address this matter on social
media? If the motive is anything other than the glory
of God and the good of others (Matt. 22:36–40), such
as a smug sense of satisfaction—the attitude of "I'm
right, and you're wrong"—then once again, pride will
press you to blurt it out. Beware, pride is skilled at
disguising itself.

Also, when guarding a prison, you are trying to
keep people from entering to help prisoners escape.
To guard your heart diligently is to prevent, as much
as possible, evil outside influences from entering
your heart, which will feed and stir up the sin that
is already there. A couple of verses later in Proverbs
4:25–27, we read, "Let your eyes look straight ahead,
and your eyelids look right before you. Ponder the

path of your feet, and let all your ways be established. Do not turn to the right or the left; remove your foot from evil." Carefully and wisely choosing what your eyes see, where your feet take you, and what your ears hear greatly aids in controlling your heart. If you are having a problem with an untamed spirit, consider what possible outward influences may be accentuating this tendency. Could it be social media itself, where untamed spirits abound? Maybe less time on social media will help. "Do not be deceived: 'Evil company corrupts good habits'" (1 Cor. 15:33). Be diligent not to unnecessarily expose yourself to things, sources, and people that have a corrupting influence on your heart. It works the other way, too—good in, good out. Expose yourself to and imitate better examples (Phil. 4:8–9).

Your Speech Is Timely

Have you ever heard the saying "Timing is everything"? It might not be everything, but wisdom is knowing when it is time to speak and when it is time to be silent, no matter how much one may know about an issue. "Even a fool is counted wise when he holds his peace; when he shuts his lips, he is considered perceptive" (Prov. 17:28). Your timing in communicating can make a huge difference in terms of receptivity and effectiveness. Of course, inquiring minds want to know, When is the right time? It would be nice to have an exhaustive list of rules to instruct us when to speak and when to keep our lips sealed, but it depends on the circumstances. Still, Proverbs gives us divine guidance on this as well.

First, it is best to communicate something only after you have given serious consideration to what you are going to say. An immediate response is almost always unwise. Proverbs 29:20 instructs us, "Do you see a man hasty in his words? There is more hope for a fool than for him." In contrast, "The heart of the righteous studies how to answer, but the mouth of the wicked pours forth evil" (Prov. 15:28). *Studies* is the Hebrew word that is sometimes translated *meditate*, which literally means "to mutter." It is a low muffle, sort of like talking under one's breath. Have you ever planned out what you are going to say to someone by actually saying it out loud in private? That's the idea of *studying* how to answer. Especially when a matter is provocative or potentially explosive, it is wise to think carefully through each word, each phrase, and even the word order, seeking to discern how it will come across to others and the reactions it might produce. This is the complete opposite of the approach of the fool, who opens the floodgates of his lips to pour forth evil. *Evil* can be translated *harmful*. The foolish communicator does not care how his words might affect others, even if the result is harm. Therefore, the fool is not concerned with timing.

Second, the right time to communicate is when the words you have carefully chosen will most likely accomplish what you intend. "A word fitly spoken is like apples of gold in settings of silver" (Prov. 25:11). That, no doubt, can include not only the choice of words and the way we speak them but also the circumstances (when and where). When we communicate at the right time and place, we are more likely to invite a good response. An example of this is in the very next verse: "Like an earring of gold and an ornament of fine gold is a wise rebuker to an obedient ear" (Prov. 25:12). A good, solid scriptural rebuke may be in order and the words chosen may be good, but a wise rebuker also chooses the best *circumstances* for the rebuke. Is it wisest to offer a rebuke to someone in the presence of others? Generally, no (Matt. 18:15)—though it may be necessary in certain circumstances (Gal. 2:11; 1 Tim. 5:20). Unnecessarily embarrassing an individual will generally not result in an obedient ear. Should you call the person and do it over the phone right before they go to work? Probably not. Your poor choice of circumstances may so offend the person that your fine choice of words will not truly be heard and considered.

I cannot say with absolute dogmatism that it is always wrong to give a rebuke, general or specific, on social media. Perhaps there are situations when it is appropriate. However, is it usually wise? No. Electronic rebukes do not bear much, if any, fruit, because social media is not the best circumstance. How effective is it to reprove sin on social media? Do you imagine hundreds of people putting down their computers, dropping to their knees, confessing their sins, and mending their ways? The reason it is ineffective is not primarily because people do not want to hear the truth. It is because when people receive communication suddenly and unexpectedly, and especially if they feel targeted publicly, they are apt to dig in their heels and turn a deaf ear to what was said. How many people do you know who have changed their positions on an issue because of a social media post?

Third, the right time to communicate is when it is fairly certain you can win the argument. "Do not go hastily to court; for what will you do in the end, when your neighbor has put you to shame?" (Prov. 25:8). The idea is not to be quick to quarrel with someone, because that person might win the argument and put you to shame. This appeals to our self-interest. It is kind of like saying, You don't want to look stupid, do you? Then do not be quick to get into an argument.

If for some reason, you believe that you have a good reason to address something on social media, you should make sure you have all the relevant data, are prepared for the counterarguments, and are ready to show how they are false. If not, be assured that there is probably someone in cyberspace who has been waiting for someone to post the position you hold. Such a person has done their homework and is prepared for battle. If you have any uncertainty about being thoroughly prepared to defend your position to the bitter end, then it is better not to enter into the argument.

A meme with a clever statement or a Bible verse is not enough to win. When we enter quickly into an argument and are made to look foolish because of our lack of preparation, we hurt the cause of truth, giving those who oppose the truth more reason to discredit it. When this happens on social media, the effect is multiplied, because so many people see it.

Fourth, communicating at the right time consists in knowing when to pull back and stop when things are getting unnecessarily heated. "The beginning of strife is like releasing water; therefore, stop contention before a quarrel starts" (Prov. 17:14). We have all witnessed a discussion turn into a verbal fight. At a particular point, things begin to spiral out of control, quickly leading to accusations and name-calling, and then relationships are impaired. Before it is over, the issue that was being discussed is not the issue anymore. Regrettably, we are usually able to identify that point after things have blown up and the damage is done. Wisdom is the ability to identify that point either before it starts or just as it begins so it can be stopped. "It is honorable for a man to stop striving, since any fool can start a quarrel" (Prov. 20:3). The result is that a measure of peace will still exist, though there may be opposing views on the matter. When Christians lack this wisdom and quarrel on social media, it is a bad testimony for the gospel. It is much better when a believer has enough wisdom and grace to say, "This is getting out of hand. Let's get together for coffee, or give me a call, and we can talk about this. I love you." That does a lot more for the advancement of truth and righteousness than winning a public argument on social media.

Admittedly, discerning when our spirit is tame and our speech is timely can be difficult. The good news is that we are not called upon to make that determination alone. You might be totally convinced that your spirit is controlled, that you have chosen good and effective words, and that the timing is right, even having prayed about it. This is why we need a warning like Proverbs 28:26: "He who trusts in his own heart is a fool, but whoever walks wisely will be delivered." Even the regenerate and good hearts of believers are not to be trusted. Too much remaining sin exists in them, which usually causes us to have a better opinion of ourselves than we should (Rom. 12:3). This is why an aspect of walking wisely is to seek out wise counsel. "The way of a fool is right in his own eyes, but he who heeds counsel is wise" (Prov. 12:15). The foolish person is satisfied with his own assessment and usually counts any input that contradicts it as wrong. Proverbs 18:1 confirms this by saying, "A man who isolates himself seeks his own desire; he rages against all wise judgment." Such a one isolates himself from the wise judgments of others because "a fool has no delight in understanding, but in expressing his own heart" (Prov. 18:2). All the fool cares about is having an opportunity to broadcast his opinion. So, he does not seek counsel before he expresses what he believes to be right.

If you regularly post on social media regarding sensitive and controversial issues, how often do you seek counsel from wise and trusted believers rather than trusting your own heart before you act? I am not asking how often you have sought confirmation. Seeking confirmation is only asking for advice from those whom you know will tell you what you want to hear. Seeking counsel is opening yourself to someone with your lips taped together and your hands tied behind your back, sincerely wanting them to "give it to you straight." If you want to ensure that the person is not merely giving you confirmation, you can always seek counsel from more than one person (Prov. 11:14). Perhaps you think if you always seek counsel before you post something that might be provocative, then the opportunity to speak to the situation will pass you by and it will not be as relevant. Exactly! That's the point. Taking the necessary time to pray for wisdom (James 1:5) and seek counsel protects us against the immediate and quick response that social media allows and invites. Test yourself. Are you willing to be humble enough to ask some trusted and wise believers to give you regular feedback about your use of social media? I might add that if you find yourself in constant need of counsel in this regard, you should probably rethink your entire approach to social media.

Chapter 2

AM I CALM?

Each of us, no matter his or her temperament, can get upset. But we each have different thresholds. It doesn't take much for some of us to reach the boiling point. Others take longer. Whatever that point is for each of us, Proverbs makes it clear that communicating while hot and in a heated manner is usually ineffective. It often does the exact opposite of what you are trying to accomplish. As you reflect on your use of social media, ask yourself, Am I calm? If you are calm in your use of social media, then two things are true: your manner is soothing, and your manner is swaying.

Your Manner Is Soothing

What is our natural reflex reaction when someone unleashes their anger against us? It is to speak harshly back to that person with raised decibels. It is so easy to let someone's anger and harshness light our fuse and set off the fireworks. Proverbs 15:1 states, "A soft answer turns away wrath, but a harsh word stirs up anger." Keep in mind that many of the Proverbs are truisms. A truism is something that usually holds true in most situations, but not 100 percent of the time. In fact, there are times when a calm response will only make the other person angrier, because they were hoping to see you lose your temper. Furthermore, this proverb is not forbidding us to respond to someone in a firm and straightforward manner or, if need be, with a raised voice. However, as a general rule (truism), a softer approach is like pouring a bucket of cold water on the other person's anger. It is disarming.

Anger is continually expressed on social media. My guess is that this, at least in part, is an effort to bring about "change." People think that if they communicate in a fiery manner, it will draw more attention to their words. Indeed, it does. Maybe you are thinking, Yes, I am fiery, but when I post "red hot" stuff, I get lots of likes and responses. But think humbly and soberly about the kind of attention it receives. Who "likes" it? I am certain the positive responses come from those who already agree with you. They are your cheerleading squad. I am certain none of the likes come from new converts who have just been won over by your arguments. Some of the comments may come from your opponents, whom you were hoping would come to the truth but who have only dug in their heels more deeply, refusing to budge. I know, I know! Don't we need to speak the truth with boldness? Yes. But don't mistake rudeness for boldness. Realize it is not always the truth people are rejecting. Sometimes a person cannot get past the poor packaging even to consider the truth. We might think people should accept the truth regardless of the packaging. Personally, however, I believe God made us to be more receptive to the truth when it is presented in certain ways, even the truth of His Word.

Your Manner Is Swaying

To *sway* is to persuade. Calm, gentle communication is generally much more persuasive than angry, harsh, matter-of-fact, or in-your-face communication. "The wise in heart will be called prudent, and sweetness of the lips increases learning" (Prov. 16:21). Honey attracts better than vinegar. Proverbs 16:24 says, "Pleasant words are like a honeycomb, sweetness to the soul and health to the bones." When people feel attacked or belittled, they tend to immediately stop listening and not give serious consideration to what you have to say. Even if what is said is accurate information or the truth of God's Word, if it has been dipped in vinegar, people will spit it out. Some Christians count being unfriended or blocked as a badge of honor. This is sad because it is a nasty spirit of self-righteousness, which interprets that as suffering for righteousness's sake when, in reality, their provocative communication is usually carnality disguised as faithfulness to the truth. If this describes you and how you have been addressing and responding to issues on social media, opt for the better and more effective way of calm and nonabrasive communication. A gentle, kind, and sweet approach goes a long way in opening people's ears and hearts to hear and accept what is true and reasonable.

Does this mean we must never say hard things? No. Things that are hard to hear and hard to accept must be communicated at times. But hard things can be said with great effect when said in soft ways. We tend to think that if someone's heart needs to be broken, strong force is required. Not so. "By long forbearance a ruler is persuaded, and a gentle tongue breaks a bone" (Prov. 25:15). I love that verse because it basically says, "Do you want to influence people in positions of authority so they will come to the truth and do the right thing? Then be long-suffering and do not use a barbed tongue." Have you ever experienced someone communicating to you in a soft way without a hint of harshness, and it broke a bone? Their words went beneath the skin and humbled you to the dust, bringing you to your proverbial knees. Even though their soft words put you in a cast for six weeks, you found it almost impossible to be angry. It hurt so good that you almost offered them another bone to break. That's heavenly wisdom in action. Ask the Lord for the wisdom and grace to communicate in this calm and sweet manner, as it is usually much more persuasive than angry and abrasive speech.

Another thing to consider in this vein is that emotions are contagious. When you have a free moment, go on the internet and look up the *Laughing Record*. It starts out slowly, and it eventually breaks out into full laughter. You will even hear a snort. No reason is given for the laughter, but I started laughing by simply listening to it.* This elevated my mood for several minutes. A person's attitude and emotional state can be passed on to others, and what is true of laughter is also true of anger. "Make no friendship with an angry man, and with a furious man do not go, lest you learn his ways and set a snare for your soul" (Prov. 22:24–25). It has become popular to rant on social media, and I am afraid that by association, people are learning to be angry. Ask yourself, Is the anger others are exhibiting on social media stirring me up to anger? Ask yourself, Is my anger sparking anger in others? What are others learning about a God-honoring, Christlike emotional life from your use of social media?

I do believe there is such a thing as righteous anger, and I cannot, in good conscience, say it should never be expressed on social media. However, if we are self-aware, we know all too well how easy it is to excuse sinful anger by labeling it as righteous anger. The apostle James instructs us, "So, then, my beloved brethren, let every man be swift to hear, slow to speak, slow to wrath; for the wrath of man does not produce

---

*I remember Al Martin, former pastor of Trinity Baptist Church, using the *Laughing Record* to make this point in one of his pastoral theology lectures for the Trinity Ministerial Academy. He was addressing the matter of emotions in preaching.

the righteousness of God" (James 1:19–20). Unrighteous anger is eager and ready to fire off a response, whereas righteous anger is usually a delayed response after one has given serious consideration to the situation (Neh. 5:6–7). I plead with you to be discerning and realize that some may intentionally dangle bait on social media in order to provoke an angry response. Sadly, some people think watching others become unglued is a form of entertainment. James tells us in no uncertain terms that it is not funny, for it does not bring about the righteous purposes of God. In fact, one way to discern if your anger is sinful or righteous is to prayerfully ask yourself, What righteous purpose will this accomplish? Even if the emotion welling up in you is indeed righteous anger, righteous anger does not express itself merely for the sake of expressing itself. That is to say, righteous anger doesn't just vent. Since righteous anger always has a righteous purpose in view, a person might hold back the expression of it when a righteous purpose is unlikely to be accomplished.

Perhaps an illustration will help you understand. Imagine that you are attending your neighbor's funeral. You have lived on the same block with him for decades. You have never met anyone as cranky and unkind in your life. He was a continual thorn in your side, yet you attend his funeral to be a good neighbor. As you listen to the minister give the eulogy, you are shocked to learn you had been living next to the apostle Paul all those years. You guessed it. The preacher preaches that unconverted man right into heaven. You are angry, and rightfully so, as many are hearing and perhaps being led astray by the false gospel that R.C. Sproul referred to as "justification by death." However, should you jump up in the middle of the service denouncing the false prophet? No. Why not? Beyond the fact that it would be inappropriate to take the floor demanding to be heard, the circumstances (look back to chapter 1) would not allow you to fully explain yourself so as to accomplish a righteous purpose. You would likely only cause confusion. Likewise, is an angry couple of lines on social media, or even a short paragraph, effective in accomplishing the righteous purposes of God? Is social media a good and effective venue to express righteous anger? Those are legitimate questions we must consider.

I want to make a heartfelt appeal to older saints and to pastors who use social media on a regular basis. Please do not become an "angry old man." Don't become a pastor with a jagged edge. Be an example to the believers (1 Tim. 4:12) by a wise and Christlike use of social media. Be calm.

Chapter 3

AM I CAREFUL?

Let me introduce you to John Doe. Mr. Doe is a Christian man who believes he has a lot of insight and should be heard. The problem is that his pastors will not give him proper recognition and opportunities to do this in church. He is frustrated that the people in the pews do not take him seriously. Then, along comes social media, and now he finally has a pulpit to fulfill his stewardship. It seems that many people have embraced the mistaken notion that social media has given them a platform where they can be heard. The humbling reality, however, is that most of us do not have a stewardship from God to communicate the truth regarding any matter via social media. If you think you have such a stewardship, more than likely it is only an inflated view of your importance. That is not meant to be harsh. It is meant as a reality check that I have had to apply to myself. I am a local pastor of a small church in a cul-de-sac. I am relatively unknown. I am certainly not among the Who's Who in the evangelical world. Therefore, I am confident that people are not sitting at home on their computers or with their smartphones in hand waiting for Jeff Johnson to speak truth about the latest issue. Thus, I feel no pressure at all, no sense of stewardship whatsoever, to use social media as a platform to herald my insights and engage others about various matters.

Does this mean we may use social media to address issues only when there is a sense of stewardship? No. Scripture nowhere teaches that we may speak about matters and engage others on issues only when we are obligated to do so. We may do so even when it is not our stewardship. So, what I would like to do in this chapter is to lay out a principle that should be applied when it is *not* your stewardship. A good way to apply this principle is to ask yourself, Am I careful? This question reflects an emphasis from Proverbs that an essential element of wisdom is calculating the potential risks and considering the possible reactions before we act in order to determine if it is worth it.

Calculate the Potential Risks

Obedience to our Lord involves taking risks in this fallen world. For example, we may risk a friendship by faithfully speaking the truth to someone we love (Prov. 27:6). We may risk a painful disruption in family relations by being loyal to Christ (Matt. 10:34–36). Calculating such risks so that we may avoid them will inevitably result in compromise. However, a key aspect of wisdom is, in certain cases, to calculate the risks of our actions before we take them. A couple of risks we each need to consider in our use of social media are that of a ruined field and a ruined family.

A Ruined Field

Calculate the risk of a ruined field. "He who tills his land will be satisfied with bread, but he who follows frivolity is devoid of understanding" (Prov. 12:11). The first half of this proverb presents us with a man who is diligently plowing and planting. Such a man will not lack for sustenance. His hard work will pay off. The second half of the verse describes the man who is wasting his time doing something else when he should be working his field. He will regret it later when there is no food on the table. His wife and children will not be happy either. The broader principle here is that we are not to waste our time and energy on unproductive pursuits, especially when they take us away from what is clearly our present duty. A worthless thing is something that is empty or vain. But even when something is worthy of attention, it can still be worthless if it distracts us from our present responsibilities. That's the principle embedded in the proverb, and it has direct application to social media. A current issue being plastered all over social media may be worthy of someone's time and energy, but is it worth yours in light of all the fields God has given you to cultivate? Examine yourself to see if social media is distracting you from the stewardships the Lord has clearly given to you.

What about the field of your marriage? I have in mind the man whose marriage is substandard. Lots of rocks are in that field, and it is producing very little fruit. I can see him sitting at his computer in a room apart from his wife with his eyes glued to the screen researching the latest controversy so he can evaluate what is being said on social media and respond intelligently. If the truth be told, he has not researched his wife in years. He is more interested in a governmental conspiracy behind vaccines. Those matters have his attention, not his bride. Consequently, more thorns and thistles are growing in the field. Sir, how is spending that time on social media helping you to love your wife like Christ loved the church? What about the field of your children? Do you know how each of them is fairing educationally and, most importantly, spiritually? Are you shepherding their souls, pointing them to Christ, preparing them to live in an unbelieving world? If you are not shaping them, trust me, someone else is doing it, and you will probably not like the finished product. If they have followed your example, their teacher is probably electronic. The fact that you know so much about the effectiveness or ineffectiveness of masks related to COVID-19 may not mean that much to you when, later, you are grieving over children who were left to themselves. To the housewife, I ask, How is the condition of your home? It is your domain. It is your field. Is social media a constant drain on faithfulness to your stewardship as a wife and mother? Is there a pile of laundry continually on the living room floor? How many projects around the house are not getting done because you can't put down your phone? Are you busy firing off on social media when duty calls? I am not suggesting that spending time on social media is wrong or the cause of a bad marriage, children who stray, or a messy house. I am only encouraging you to consider how it might be a distraction from your responsibilities.

Dear pastor, how is the field of your ministerial labors? I anticipate that pastor who would tell me he checks his social media account several times a day, posting and commenting as he goes. But he is also quick to tell me that it is only for a few minutes at a time. No big deal, right? Personally, I think that it is beneficial for a pastor to be on social media since it can keep him informed of what society and the people in the pews see as the pressing issues of the day. This can have a positive effect on his preaching and counseling as he tries to make relevant applications to the members of the church. He might enjoy doing internet searches on issues and interacting at some level about those issues on social media. Such can be a healthy diversion from the pressures of the ministry. Let's not go the way of hyperspirituality, believing that a pastor must have no interests other than his calling. It comes down to each man knowing himself and his own tendencies. My point is that you may be

surprised at how many hours those few-minute inter-
vals throughout the day add up to over the period of a
year. Consider how much time you potentially waste
on social media, including the amount of time you are
distracted with thoughts about what you have read
or how you should respond even when you are not
online. Think of the negative impact this distraction
could be having on sermon preparation. How much
more gospel fruit would your ministerial field yield if
those few minutes throughout the day were dedicated
to prayer for your church members and lost souls in
need of Christ? Think of the good that could be done
if, instead of responding to someone else's post, you
called to check on an elderly saint. Please, my dear
brother, don't underestimate how much effectiveness
social media can steal from your ministry.

How is the field of your own soul? This may
sound counterintuitive, but we need to be cautious
even about constantly listening to or viewing sermons
online. Really? Really! I am not at all suggesting that
we can get too much Scripture, and I am sure that
we could all benefit from listening to additional sermons. But there is a difference between listening to
additional messages for the edification of your own
soul and listening to sermon after sermon in order
to acquire more weapons to fight for your cause on
social media.

More examples could be given, but I trust you
get the point. Prayerfully consider if social media

has become an idol at whose altar you are making a multitude of daily sacrifices. Survey your fields. Are any of them headed to ruin for the sake of this electronic god?

A Ruined Family

Calculate the risk of a ruined family. I am not referring to your earthly family. I am talking about the family of God. As I mentioned at the beginning of the book, social media has become a means of great division among Christians, not only among those who know one another distantly but also among believers in the local church. Such division can do long-term damage. We do well to take seriously the warning of Proverbs 18:19: "A brother offended is harder to win than a strong city, and contentions are like the bars of a castle." It is possible to so offend your brother that it is easier to conquer a city than to regain his affections. He may be so deeply offended that he has put up mental and emotional walls, and no matter how hard you try to regain his affections, he will not let you. "That's not right," someone exclaims. "The offended brother shouldn't be that way, especially if I am humbly and sincerely seeking forgiveness." Okay, fine. Do not assume this proverb is giving approval to the brother being hardened against you. Instead, it is simply telling us what is. The book of Proverbs is inspired realism. It deals with life as it really is without sugarcoating it. This proverb presents us with the cold facts of how deeply we can offend a brother or sister in the Lord. I fear that if Christians do not "turn the curve" and begin using social media more wisely, more of us will come to church with invisible but real walls around our hearts because of something another brother or sister has communicated on social media. The result will be less and less real, open-hearted communion with one another. Sadly, over time, some will determine that it is in their best interest to start afresh in another church where they can slowly let the walls down, in an attempt to build new and healthy relationships. When deciding to communicate on social media, ask yourself, Is this worth the risk of alienating my brother? A person has a rotten attitude when they think it does not matter as long as they are "speaking the truth." Isn't love supposed to be somewhere in that equation (Eph. 4:15)? Is it really worth the risk of setting off a chain reaction that could ruin the local family of God?

Consider the Possible Reactions

As the salt and light of the world (Matt. 5:13–16), believers have the responsibility to influence this godless world toward God and righteousness. Communicating God's truth is an integral part of that responsibility. Modern technology is a blessing in that regard, because it gives us the opportunity to disseminate truth more quickly and broadly than ever before. Nothing I write in this book should be taken as a prohibition of spreading the knowledge of truth and righteousness electronically, not even when it comes to social media. However, the purpose of this book is to help us think carefully about how biblical principles of communication should guide us in our use of social media. One biblical principle to guide us in discerning whether or not we should speak out for truth and righteousness in a given situation is that we are to carefully consider the possible reactions.

Beware of Fangs

Self-preservation is not exclusively driven by sinful motives. A concern for your own good is an essential part of wisdom. For example, we read in Proverbs 26:17, "He who passes by and meddles in a quarrel not his own is like one who takes a dog by the ears." A puppy might be sweet as honey and super cuddly. He might be very playful, nipping at you as though he would tear you apart. Grab him by the ears, though. I dare you! I don't mean rub his ears. I mean grab them and pull. You are not going to do that, because you don't want to get bit. That's what can happen when you stick your nose where it doesn't belong. You intruded into a debate or conversation on social media to offer your point of view. That's when it happened. You got bit. You were hurt and upset because you were "only trying to help." But the truth of the matter is you got bit because you were meddling where you were neither wanted nor needed. The proverb says you should have minded your own business. Always determine if your unsolicited input is worth the risk of some teeth marks!

Beware of Fools
Consider your audience. It is one thing to communicate to those who are genuinely interested in the truth and want to hear it. Even if they are not yet agreeable to the truth, at least they will give you a fair and honest hearing. The objections of such people, even if illogical, tend to be genuine interactions. When such people challenge you and your position, it can help you sharpen your mental skills and tighten up the loose ends of your arguments.

Not all people who challenge you, though, are genuine in their responses. Some people have their guns loaded, ready to fire at any presentation of the truth, no matter how airtight the arguments. And quite frankly, it is not worth your time or sanity to engage them. Proverbs 23:9 says, "Do not speak in the hearing of a fool, for he will despise the wisdom of your words." This does not mean, of course, that we are to communicate the truth only to those who are receptive to it. How else will the fool become wise if no one ever speaks the truth to him? We are not to speak to the fool when it is evident that all the fool wants to do is strive, rail against the truth, and make fun of it. "If a wise man contends with a foolish man, whether the fool rages or laughs, there is no peace" (Prov. 29:9).

The fool will go round after round with you, and this gets you nowhere. The belief that we are to disseminate God's truth indiscriminately among men without any consideration of their responses is not true. The Lord Jesus Himself warns, "Do not give what is holy to the dogs; nor cast your pearls before swine, lest they trample them under their feet, and turn and tear you in pieces" (Matt. 7:6). We are to remain silent when a person begins to trample the truth and attack us, even when they twist the truth to use it against us.

On the other hand, Proverbs 26:4–5 instructs us, "Do not answer a fool according to his folly, lest you also be like him. Answer a fool according to his folly, lest he be wise in his own eyes." On the one hand, we are not to lower ourselves to the fool's level of arguing and striving. When we do, the fool has won by making us be like him. Instead, we are to speak to the fool when we can show him the foolishness of his beliefs and arguments, in hopes that his eyes and heart will be opened to the truth. Answering the fool "according to his folly" can at times include some "sanctified sarcasm" and "holy harshness" (1 Kings 18:26–27; Matt. 23:13–33). However, effective arguments for the truth are well thought out, carefully crafted from the Scriptures, and delivered in an orderly manner. This is the art of persuasion. This takes time (Acts 17:1–12), and therein is the application that needs to be made to social media. The immediacy and brevity that social media demands make social media a playground for the fool, because it offers him a platform to broadcast curt and vitriolic proclamations of his beliefs, with little to no reasoning or verification of facts. Christians need to consider seriously if we are allowing social media to dictate the way we communicate, molding us into the likeness of the fool.

Be careful!

Chapter 4

AM I COMPASSIONATE?

How things have changed! When I was a boy, the local news came on at six o'clock in the evening and again at eleven. Additionally, there may have been an early morning local news show. National news came on once a day, immediately following the six o'clock broadcast. Local and national newspapers and news magazines existed as well. That was about it. Then cable news channels came along, and now, with news talk shows, the expansion of the internet, and the invention of smartphones, we can literally get news 24 hours a day, 365 days a year. We can access local, national, and world news at any time and at any place. An incident can occur, and the whole world can know about it in minutes. News travels even faster now because social media has given us the ability to send it to hundreds and thousands of people with the touch of a few buttons.

This has led to much confusion and error regarding the virtue of compassion. When a news story regarding some tragedy or especially some form of injustice is hot off the press, people post these stories on their social media accounts, accompanied by their commentary and personal views. Those who supposedly excel in the virtue of compassion are able to wax eloquent, writing posts with great, heartfelt insight. This sets off a chain reaction of responses, many of which are supportive, expressing thanks and appreciation and applauding the person for speaking out. Some of the responses are negative and challenge the person, but the warrior for compassion will not back down as he demonstrates what an advocate he is for the victims, the suffering, and the less fortunate. Other people are well-known for speaking out on social media regarding certain issues. You can be assured that they will respond to an incident by condemning the offender(s), supporting the victim(s), and correcting all who do not have a correct or biblical view of the incident.

This can be confusing for Christians because there seems to be either direct or subtle pressure to respond to these sad and tragic events, perhaps even on social media. To be "silent" or inactive is interpreted by some as being in league with the perpetrators, cowardice, or at least sinful indifference. Some digital soldiers of compassion express their disappointment and disgust at professing Christians for not taking a public stand. They're deeply troubled at how many professing Christians are unlike Christ. They wish others cared as much as they do. All of this can make us feel guilty and inadequate, because, apparently, we must not have the spiritual maturity and strength necessary to spread compassion in the world. This can also be quite overwhelming, because it is hard to keep up with all the bad and sad news being funneled through social media. No sooner does one incident fade into the background than a new one arises, and we better be on the compassion bandwagon for that one, too. Posting articles or videos of past injustices has become a trend, and you are made to believe that something is wrong with you if it does not make you feel bad. You better not say anything that even sounds like the "I had nothing to do with that injustice" attitude—that is, if you don't want to be publicly rebuked before the watching eyes of social media. Again, all this can be confusing to the average Christian, leaving him or her asking the question, Am I compassionate?

Willful ignorance concerning evil and injustice can be a problem. I want to be clear that I am not promoting in this book quietism or passivism, where Christians are simply to sit on padded pews and trust God working His sovereign will, while wickedness flourishes and people suffer. Such is an inexcusable perversion of the Christian faith. Each of us must discern what role we have in exposing and resisting evil and coming to the aid of the oppressed. "Deliver those who are drawn toward death, and hold back those stumbling to the slaughter. If you say, 'Surely we did not know this,' does not He who weighs the hearts consider it? He who keeps your soul, does He not know it? And will He not render to each man according to his deeds?" (Prov. 24:11–12). However, social media is not a good tool to discern the measure of a person's compassion. If we are going to make sense of compassion in this digital age, then we need to distinguish the true compassion of the righteous and the false compassion of the wicked. Consider this proverb that gets to the heart of the matter: "A righteous man regards the life of his animal, but the tender mercies of the wicked are cruel" (Prov. 12:10). "Tender mercies" is one word in the original Hebrew text, and it can be translated *compassion*. Now, that is interesting! How can compassion ever be cruel? Isn't any degree of compassion a good thing? Obviously, what is meant is that the compassion of the wicked is not real compassion. It appears on the surface to be compassion, but it is actually a form of cruelty. In contrast, this proverb reveals that true compassion is *practical*, and most often, true compassion is *private*.

Compassion Is Practical

The first part of the proverb says that the righteous man cares about his animals (beasts of burden). He feeds and waters them every day and nurses them when they're sick. How much more practical can you get? The righteous man shows his compassion in practical, hands-on ways in the course of his daily responsibilities. In contrast, the false compassion of the wicked is impractical, in that it usually tends to be all talk. It is cruelty because sympathy is expressed for those in need while nothing is done to help relieve their suffering (James 2:15–16). Social media promotes this type of false compassion, which can lead us to self-deception. We can mistakenly think that because we saw a picture or a news story, had an emotional reaction to it, and called upon others to share it on social media, we are excelling in the virtue of compassion. In reality, we have done nothing practical to help. In fact, in many cases, we are incapable of doing anything about it, due to several factors: the incident or problem is in the past, and nothing can be done about it; or it took place in a distant state or on the other side of the world, and we have no practical way of being involved; or it is unrealistic for us to be involved, because our schedule and commitments preclude us from "taking up the cause" in a hands-on way. If any of those three things are true, what practical value exists in broadcasting human suffering on social media, informing people how much you care, or responding to those posts with "likes" or "sad faces"? I realize the legitimacy of posting things in order to call people to prayer, particularly in cases of local and national tragedies. But beware of how social media can be a breeding ground for the useless false compassion of the wicked. Do not be led astray by it.

Contrast this with the compassion we find in Christ, as recorded in the gospel accounts of His life and ministry. Most passages of Scripture that reveal our Savior's compassion include three elements: recognition, reaction, and relief (e.g., Matt. 9:36–38; Luke 7:13–14). *Recognition*: He saw some form of human suffering. *Reaction*: He had an emotional response. *Relief*: He took action to relieve the suffering. Jesus's deep emotional reaction always moved Him to take action. His compassion was *practical*. It was demonstrated in the context of His daily life and ministry to those who providentially came across His path, and He taught us to do the same in the parable of the good Samaritan (Luke 10:25–37). I assume that the Samaritan was having a typical day when he found a man lying on the side of the Jericho Road, beaten and half dead. The opportunity to show compassion came to him in God's providence while he lived out his everyday life. When it did, he did not organize a march to raise awareness for the lives lost on the Jericho Road. Like Jesus, he had an emotional reaction to what he saw, which moved him to bring relief to the sufferer in the most practical of ways. That is real compassion. The priest and Levite were not condemned because they did not leave supportive comments and draw sad faces beside the dying man's body. Their sin was that they did not offer practical assistance.

Understanding this can help relieve false guilt for those who feel the pressure to take up every cause promoted via social media. I just cannot care about so much stuff at once. My heart is just not big enough to contain it all. I am not obligated to feel deeply about and respond to all human suffering and every injustice at the same time and to the same degree. Neither are you. That is not how the virtue of compassion works. It does not mean you are not compassionate just because you have not read that book someone gave you in hopes that you would become more aware. Nor is your lack of interest in reading it an indicator that you would rather remain blissfully ignorant so that you can go on undisturbed with your nice middle-class suburban life. And it does not mean you are not compassionate just because the documentary you watched, which was suggested on social media, did not make you cry. Whether you are compassionate is found in how you—like the righteous man in the proverb, who cared for his animals—respond to real needs that come within the context of your everyday life and responsibilities. Also, realize that those who are the most vehement in publicly condemning others for not being compassionate are not always quite as compassionate as they make themselves out to be (John 12:3–6).

Does this mean Christians are not to be involved in causes that are outside their daily responsibilities? I am not saying that at all. A Christian *may* be involved in such causes, and at times, a Christian *ought* to be involved. When it is good for a Christian to be involved and when it is his duty to be involved depend on various factors, and it would take us beyond the scope of my concern to address that matter. However, if a person is taking up a cause while bypassing opportunities to show compassion to those in the path of his daily responsibilities, then his "compassion" is probably soiled with impure motives.

Compassion Is Private

Referring back to the proverb, we can ask, How many people see the man taking care of his animals? Maybe his wife and children. Maybe a neighbor. People do not gather in big crowds to cheer him on as he goes about this daily chore. No one will write a blog about this amazing display of compassion. I suggest that the picture of the righteous man caring for his animals may also teach us that acts of true compassion are usually private. In contrast, the false compassion of the wicked is a kind of compassion in which the benefactors openly parade their "goodness." Though people's needs are met to some degree, it is cruel nonetheless, because the sufferings and injustices of others are used for self-glory. Jesus warned us about this false compassion when He forbade us to do our righteous deeds to be seen by men, exposing the hypocrisy of the scribes and Pharisees, who called attention to themselves when they gave to the poor and needy (Matt. 6:1–4). They did not truly care about others. They were glory seekers who desired the praise of men for being such fine specimens of compassion.

What greater and more effective way exists to parade our righteousness before the eyes of men than the global network of social media? With just a click of a button, we can let hundreds or thousands of people know about our heart for justice, for victims, and for those in need. We can also let others know what we are doing to make a difference. Our Lord clearly taught us that we are to do such deeds privately, with a single-eyed focus to please our heavenly Father, who will reward us openly in His time and in His way (Matt. 6:4). He even said that we are to perform such acts of compassion with a measure of self-imposed forgetfulness (v. 3), lest in dwelling on the good deed, we congratulate ourselves. This does not mean we are forbidden from doing public acts of compassion (5:16). Jesus did many Himself. The Lord Jesus is addressing our motives and laying down the principle that, as a general rule, the louder (6:2) we are about how much we care, and the more visible we intentionally are to others, the more likely we are seeking glory from men. We need to be constantly on guard against this false form of compassion, especially since social media provides us with a way to broadcast it immediately.

We should be aware of the subtle ways in which we can be guilty of using social media in this manner. For example, you take a selfie of yourself and your family serving at the soup kitchen and post it with an appropriate hashtag. It seems innocent enough, as your caption reads, "I am so thankful for the opportunity to teach my children the importance of serving others." You post a picture of yourself with the little old lady who lives across the street. A rake is in your hand, and you make sure the pile of leaves is in the background. Why do that? Why not just obey the simple teaching of Jesus and keep it as private as possible unless there is a good and righteous reason to do otherwise? "Let another man praise you, and not your own mouth; a stranger, and not your own lips" (Prov. 27:2). The motive behind posting something like "Today, I am burdened and praying for…" might be totally pure, since even the apostle Paul would share a portion of his prayer life with others for their encouragement (Phil. 1:3–5). However, we need to be mindful that our Lord warned us about scratching our itch for self-glory in this area as well (Matt 6:5–6). Why not share directly and only with those for whom you are praying? Why broadcast it to hundreds of others via social media? When in doubt and when wrestling with your motives, it is best to err on the side of keeping it private. The fact is, if you are a genuine believer and consistently show compassion, others will eventually learn of it and be influenced by it (Acts 20:33–35). Let us prayerfully reflect on our use of social media in this area, taking to heart that what one does in private is the measure of his true character. True compassion is satisfied when good has been done, and the Father knows it, even if no one else ever does.

Chapter 5

AM I CONSCIENTIOUS?

It simply would not be acceptable for us to act and communicate in person the way we do on social media. Not too long ago, someone posted the following on their Facebook timeline, which humorously illustrates this point:

> I am trying to make friends outside of Facebook while applying the same principles. Therefore, every day I walk down the street and tell passers-by what I have eaten, how I feel at the moment, what I have done the night before, what I will do later and with whom. I give them pictures of my family, my dog and of me gardening, taking things apart in the garage, watering the lawn, standing in front of landmarks, driving around town, having lunch and doing what anybody and everybody does every day. I also listen to their conversations, give them "thumbs up" and tell them I like them. And it works just like Facebook! I already have four people following me: two police officers, a private investigator and a psychiatrist.*

---

*Someone posted this on Facebook. I am not sure of its origin, but it can be found in various places on the internet.

A social media platform like that lacks reality. Take the idea of Facebook friends. I have over nine hundred Facebook friends. Who has that many true friends in real life? Some of them have requested to be my friend because of their connection to someone I know, and vice versa. Those are not people with whom I have a real friendship. But it does provide a fast and easy way to end a "friendship." With just a touch of a button, we're no longer friends. Imagine doing that to someone in person. You go up to the person and say, "I just unfriended you," and then walk away. You don't have to go through the gut-wrenching process of sitting down with the person and talking through matters, explaining why the relationship must end. Also, imagine a scenario where you go up to a "friend" to start a conversation, and you are completely ignored. You've been "blocked."

Why would our consciences scream bloody murder (I hope) if we did that sort of thing to someone in person, yet we have no problem doing it on social media? Social media has created an alternate world where we do not have to act according to the principles of Scripture. The danger is that we will not be able to keep the two worlds separate much longer. Either the way we interact on social media will begin to shape the way we interact in person, or the way we interact in person will alter our behavior on social media. All this to say, how we use social media should be a matter of conscience. In the language of the apostle Paul, we should strive always to have a conscience void of offense toward God and man in this area of our lives, as in all other areas (Acts 24:16). Therefore, as you reflect upon your use of social media, ask yourself, Am I conscientious?

Your Intention Is Consecrated

The matter and manner of our communication are not all that matters to God. The real reason behind the communication matters, too. Therefore, answering yes to the question, Am I conscientious? is saying that your *intention is consecrated*. It is pure and holy. Proverbs teaches that a person's matter and manner of communication may be pure when considered objectively but impure when unseen motives are considered.

The Fake Communicator

The fake communicator is one whose matter and manner are pure, but it is all a disguise to cover the impurity of his heart. "He who hates, disguises it with his lips, and lays up deceit within himself; when he speaks kindly, do not believe him, for there are seven abominations in his heart" (Prov. 26:24–25). This is the person in whom little to no fault can be found in what he said or how he said it. His speech is commendable on the surface. "On the surface" is the key phrase. The nice, kind, and gracious words are a disguise for the sin in his heart. Though the text speaks of a person who is veiling his hatred, I believe the principle is broader, applying to any instance when we cover sinful intentions with good and kind words.

You have some nasty stuff going on in your heart toward a particular person who has upset you by something they have done, said, or posted, but you are careful not to reveal it. Your method of dealing with the person is to post something on social media that is kind and filled with scriptural wisdom but is intended as a subliminal message to set the person straight. For example, there is an issue in your church that you believe many people do not understand correctly, and you are perturbed at them. So, you post an article on the subject, knowing many of those wrongheaded people will be sure to see it and, ideally, read it. You are very careful to disguise it by introducing the article in a friendly way with something like this: "This article really helped me. I hope it is a blessing." Don't misunderstand. I realize we must use tact. It certainly wouldn't be gracious to pop people between the eyes declaring, "Some of y'all [excuse the southern expression] really need to read this." However, tactfulness is not a green light to be disingenuous. Did the article really help you, or did you immediately light up with excitement when you read it because you thought it might effectively put some people in their place? Did it send you to the throne of grace for pardon and fresh strength, or did your heart fill up with a sense of self-righteousness, because it confirmed your own understanding, making you eager to show others your superiority? This can be very subtle. It can be as subtle as "liking" someone's post, knowing some of your "friends" will see it and get the message. Perhaps this is a form of what has been labeled as *passive-aggressive*.

More examples could be given, but I trust you get the point. We must be keenly aware of this phony kind of communication and take to heart the warning that comes from the same text: "Though his hatred is covered by deceit, his wickedness will be revealed before the assembly" (Prov. 26:26). In other words, the Lord has ways of removing our façade and bringing our true attitudes and motives to the surface for many to see.

The Funny Communicator

The same goes for joking. Back up just a bit to Proverbs 26:18–19: "Like a madman who throws firebrands, arrows, and death, is the man who deceives his neighbor, and says, 'I was only joking!'" Scripture does not condemn innocent joking such as one-line zingers designed in good fun to poke at one another when it is taken as a good sport. Sometimes a funny or punny post on social media can brighten the day. This proverb condemns deceptive joking—when what is said seems meant to be only humorous but, in reality, is meant to harm. When the arrows find their marks, the one who shot them says, "Aw, I was just kidding around." It is not funny to God. It offends Him. It is deceptive to communicate something on social media using a funny twist in order to have an escape route and look innocent when people are hurt by it. I mentioned in the last chapter that sarcasm can, at times, be a legitimate rhetorical device to speak the truth. But sarcasm can also be a form of this deceptive joking, meant to disguise an attack. Do you have a clear conscience that your joking on social media is not merely a deceptive way to disguise attacks against others?

If you are like me, you live daily on the battleground of Romans 7, where, as a converted man, the apostle Paul lamented, "I find then a law, that evil is present with me, the one who wills to do good" (Rom. 7:21). One way we experience the reality of this verse is that, as believers, we know the frustration of doing something when both good and evil motives are present simultaneously. It is part of the contradiction we struggle with in our hearts. I am not so naïve as to suggest that our motives must be perfectly pure before doing something. If this were the case, we would never attempt to do anything good, because our best deeds and purest motives are tainted with sin. I do, however, want us to reflect carefully and prayerfully on our motives by bringing them under the light and scrutiny of Scripture.

Your Information Is Correct

At its core, the ninth commandment—"You shall not bear false witness against your neighbor" (Ex. 20:16)—is a prohibition against all forms of lying and deception (Prov. 19:5). Giving false testimony in a legal proceeding is one of the severest forms of lying, but the commandment establishes our obligation to communicate what is true in any and every circumstance. We all make the mistake of accidentally communicating false information. This is not necessarily a sin if we correct the error, demonstrating that we had no intention to deceive. However, what people may fail to recognize is that the ninth commandment can be violated even when there is no intention to deceive. How so?

One way this happens is when we are not careful in the way we obtain the information we pass along to others. Let me introduce you to two of my favorite proverbs, both of which are practical applications of the ninth commandment. The first one says, "He who answers a matter before he hears it, it is folly and shame to him" (Prov. 18:13). You heard something, read something, or saw something on the news, and you respond by plastering it on your social media account, pronouncing your verdict with commentary. What's wrong with that? What's wrong with it is that *you have not heard it* yet. You have heard some of it, but chances are you have not heard all of it. Are you sure there is not more to the story? This not only happens with news stories concerning events but also with supposed data regarding controversial topics. There seems to be no shortage of "data" and "here are the facts about…" articles. Isn't it loving to help people understand the facts based on the latest and most reliable scientific studies? Okay, but do you know for sure, without question, that the data is accurate? If your answer is yes, my next question is, How do you know? Did you research the sources from which that data was collected, or did you just read it and think, "That sounds right"? Be honest; did you readily accept that data simply because you wanted it to be right? Whether we want to admit it or not, the fact is, we very often accept the data that agrees with what we want to be true. This is called confirmation bias. Confirmation bias is when your investigation is subtly manipulated to reach a predetermined conclusion. You can almost always find data to support your point of view. I am not saying that it is impossible to arrive at the truth concerning a matter. But we have to be extremely cautious, humbly recognizing that each of us has a strong tendency to draw conclusions too quickly that align with our position. We think we are completely objective, but we're not—which means we must prayerfully work hard at not carelessly passing on inaccurate information.

The other proverb, which is very much related, is this: "The first one to plead his cause seems right, until his neighbor comes and examines him"

(Prov. 18:17). The first person to give his side of the story is often so convincing that you believe him completely. However, once you hear the other side of the story, you realize there is much more to it. I find it amusing when someone says, "I watched seven videos on the internet, and they all say the same thing," as though it must be true since that many videos affirm the same thing. But what about all the videos on the internet that claim the opposite? Why do you believe those sources and not the others? Any source can make mistakes, manipulate information, leave out information, or intentionally mislead. We are naïve if we think that only "liberal" sources of information do this, and "conservative" sources don't. Again, the point is not that it's hopeless to discern the truth regarding a matter. The point is that we should be extremely cautious and not unintentionally break the ninth commandment by naïvely and blindly trusting sources. The ability social media has given us to broadcast information immediately to so many at once has dramatically increased the chances of us violating the ninth commandment in this way.

We must especially be careful in the way we obtain information and pass it along when the content concerns other people. The ninth commandment is stated in such a way so as to underscore this: "You shall not bear false witness against your neighbor" (Ex. 20:16). In light of what has already been said about carelessness with the truth, consider that the

ninth commandment does not say, "Do not intentionally bear false witness against your neighbor." All it
takes, technically, to bear false witness is for the testimony to be false. The content, not just the motive,
matters to God. Consider the deterrents to giving
false testimony God set forth in the Old Testament.
Those deterrents would certainly have caused an
honest person to be extremely cautious when offering
testimony against another person in a legal proceeding. The greatest deterrent was that the false witness
was to receive the exact punishment the accused
would have received, including the death penalty
(Deut. 19:15–21). Such punishment was reserved for
those who intentionally gave false testimony. However, the penalty for bearing false witness would have
caused an honest person to be reticent to testify if he
or she had the slightest doubt concerning someone's
guilt. If the testimony was proven to be inaccurate,
how would the honest but mistaken witness prove
that the false testimony was unintentional? Facing the
prospect of such punishment would certainly make
an honest person slow to offer information about an
alleged crime. Another safeguard against bearing false
witness was making the witness cast the first stone at
the execution in a capital murder case (Deut. 17:7).
One would hope the thought of leading in an execution would cause the honest person to ponder, Did
I really see what I think I saw? How could someone
cast that first stone if they had the slightest doubt?

My point is this: Is it okay for us to be less careful with the truth on social media than we would be if called upon to be a witness in a legal proceeding? Of course not. We should *always* be extremely cautious and reserved in sharing information about other people, especially when it can damage them in some way. This is always true, even when we have no intention to deceive. There is no exception to this kind of caution, even when it concerns notoriously wicked people or unrighteous civil officials. Such people should be protected by the ninth commandment just as much as those people whom we hold in high regard. Regardless of a person's character, we should never be quick to believe and pass on an evil report without clearly and thoroughly substantiating it. A person's character can be assassinated when we are not careful with the truth on social media. I once heard a story, which is said to be folklore, about a boy who had spread an evil report concerning a good man of the town. As part of making things right, he was ordered to take a feather pillow, tear it apart, and let it fly in the wind. Afterward, he was told to go collect each feather that was in the pillow. He replied that it would be impossible to track down all those feathers. This was a lesson to teach the boy that though he was sorry for the slander, he would not be able to completely stop the negative impact of his words. Even when such information is removed soon after it is broadcasted, because of the immediate and broad audience of social media, it can still have a negative impact. "The words of a talebearer are like tasty trifles, and they go down into the inmost body" (Prov. 26:22). On the other hand, "Where there is no wood, the fire goes out; and where there is no tale-bearer, strife ceases" (v. 20).

I also want to address another violation of the ninth commandment that takes place on social media. It takes place on media at large, not just social media, and it pertains to video footage. Another stipulation God set forth as a safeguard against people giving false testimony is that a person could only be con-victed of a crime when two or three witnesses were present (Deut. 19:15). They had to actually witness the crime occur. This is a universal and unalterable principle of justice, even having application to dis-cipline in the local church (Matt. 18:15–17; 1 Tim. 5:19). Whether it is legitimate to use video footage as proof alongside multiple eyewitness testimonies, in lieu of eyewitness testimony, or to exonerate someone is not something I am prepared to address; however, I do want to address the notion that no proof of a crime could be better than what is captured on video. Consider the following reasons why this notion is mistaken and why eyewitness testimony is superior.

First, the superiority of eyewitness testimony is confirmed by the gospel message. God could have ordained video recording to be invented before His Son was born so that His life, ministry, death, and resurrection would be recorded. Copies could have been made and sent around the world. How convincing a recording would be of the stone rolling away from the tomb, the soldiers hitting the ground like dead men, and Jesus emerging alive and well! But God chose to confirm the veracity and trustworthiness of the gospel message by eyewitness testimony (Luke 1:1–4; Acts 1:21–22), and countless numbers of people have believed the report (1 Tim. 3:16). If video footage were sufficient and superior, our all-wise God would certainly have chosen that method.

Second, a video recording is two-dimensional and does not provide the perspective that can be given by multiple eyewitnesses who see and hear from several different angles. Someone might say, "Yes, but can't multiple people conspire to bear false witness?" Yes, of course. But that still does not make video footage superior and more reliable. Let's employ some common sense. If people can conspire to give false testimony, how much more can a two-dimensional, one-perspective image be altered and manipulated to tell a false story? Even if the image is not electronically altered, all it takes for the image to "bear false witness" is for news outlets to put a narrative with it and broadcast it over and over again until what they have chosen for us to believe about the incident is so deeply embedded that we are unable to believe otherwise (Prov. 26:20). The ability social media has given us to share videos broadcasted by media outlets only multiplies the potential to bear that kind of false witness. Furthermore, it is rare to have more than one video of an incident, which does not satisfy the multiple-witness standard. If another video does exist of the same incident, it can be easily withheld from the public to strengthen the narrative.

Third, images have a way of impacting us emotionally while bypassing our reason. When we see an image, especially a video of an alleged evil act, our emotions are stirred up before we even think logically, or before we consider possible alternative interpretations of the incident. Then, once the provocative image spreads to millions of people within a matter of minutes, there is a national outcry for justice, which makes it even more difficult to rationally process what we have seen. In contrast, *listening* to multiple eyewitnesses in an official legal proceeding requires you to think through their testimonies logically and rationally, processing their *words*. You must carefully determine if inconsistencies and contradictions in the testimonies exist and if the multiple witnesses agree (Mark 14:56–59). It is much easier to discharge this responsibility when you are not under the influence of provocative images, which so easily and quickly sway you one way or the other.

Therefore, the ninth commandment is severely violated when video footage of an alleged crime is broadcast over the news and social media, and a verdict is practically rendered before eyewitness testimony can be given in an official legal context. How can the alleged perpetrator receive a fair hearing and a just trial when he's already been found guilty in the court of public opinion based on video footage (John 7:51)? Most likely, all the jurors have thereby "seen" the alleged crime and have already formed a solid opinion before the trial. Also, if millions of people have already determined that the alleged perpetrator is guilty, then the jurors and judge are pressured to begin the trial leaning heavily toward a guilty verdict or potentially face the wrath of the mob (Prov. 29:8). This is one reason why I, as a pastor, do not jump into the pulpit and condemn the latest alleged crime or injustice that has been caught on camera. I refrain from doing so because it violates the ninth commandment. I agree that the populace should hold the legal system accountable. But for people, most of whom do not even live in the city where the alleged crime took place (Deut. 21:18–21), to try to do so based on video footage is unjust. The ninth commandment reveals that eyewitness testimony is God's way of establishing guilt. Let's be content with His way. His way is best.

Your Iniquity Is Confessed

I'll admit it. I do not like shame. However, shame is not always a bad thing, because shame facilitates repentance (Ezek. 16:62–63; Rom. 6:21). That is one of the major motivations behind why I post

very little on social media and why what I do post
is benign. I want to avoid public shame. Allow me
to explain. My conviction is that sin committed on
social media should be confessed on social media.
Proverbs 28:13 says, "He who covers his sins will not
prosper, but whoever confesses and forsakes them
will have mercy." To cover our sin is to fail to own
our sin and take responsibility for it. To confess and
forsake our sin is to take full responsibility for it and
be determined, by the grace of God, not to do it again.
Honestly, how often have you ever read a confession
of sin from someone on social media for something
they posted on social media? We might think, Is it not
enough to confess those sins to God? But though confession of our sin is to be primarily to God, it is not
to stop there. Our repentance is to be as wide as the
offense. This includes seeking the forgiveness of those
we have sinned against (Luke 17:3), repairing the
damage we have done when possible (Luke 19:8–10),
and making it clear that we have forsaken that sin
(2 Cor. 7:9–11). This is essential to maintaining a
clear conscience (Acts 24:16; also see Acts 23:1–3).
Therefore, sin committed on social media should be
confessed on social media. If the sin was a hidden,
undisclosed attitude that could not be detected by
others, there is no need to confess it publicly, since no
one but you and God are aware of it; however, when
your sin on social media has been against others, or is
evident to others, to confess it only to God is a cheap

way to appease your conscience, and it is a proud refusal to be humble.

Is there sin you have committed on social media that you need to confess on social media? The warning of Proverbs 28:13 is that if you cover it by a refusal to confess it, you will not prosper. Could this be the cause of a spiritual dry spell you are currently experiencing? Have you had a nagging conscience for some time that will not let you rest, and you have yet to identify the culprit? Take some time to scroll back through your social media accounts, prayerfully considering each one of your posts and interactions to see if that could be the reason. Look at each one, considering if there is sin to confess to God and to others. Some things may be old and perhaps should just be removed rather than resurrected by confession, which may cause offense to many who never saw them or who do not remember them. In such cases, it is legitimate to make a general confession that some (or many) of your posts and interactions have been sinful, that you have sought God's forgiveness, and that you are now seeking the forgiveness of those who have been offended. We do not have a comprehensive list covering every scenario regarding when it is our duty to confess our sin to others. Wise judgment needs to be applied to each case. The point is that biblical confession of sin should govern our use of social media as it should every area of life. Be encouraged by the promise of the above proverb, which promises mercy when we are willing to humble ourselves in this way.

Ecclesiastes 10:1 says, "Dead flies putrefy the perfumer's ointment, and cause it to give off a foul odor; so does a little folly to one respected for wisdom and honor." No one wants what is in the bottle, because it stinks, and the healing properties have been contaminated. Likewise, a whole lot of good can be spoiled by a little bit of foolishness. Are you held in high esteem as a mature and wise Christian who emits the sweet fragrance of your Savior? If so, do not allow social media to become the dead fly in your ointment, or people may not want the good you have to offer, because they can't get past the smell! If this has happened to you, be encouraged that confession of sin can go a long way in purifying your bottle, because humility can restore people's confidence and respect. If you discover that flies keep spoiling your ointment, one option should be considered—getting off social media altogether. This is in keeping with Scripture's emphasis on removing all occasions of temptation and sin (Matt. 5:29–30; 1 Cor. 10:13).

CONCLUSION

Every sermon I preach ultimately warrants some qualifications and balancing perspectives. The problem is that I cannot possibly make all of them in one sermon. The people have to come back week after week as those qualifications and balancing statements are made over time. The same is true of this little book. I do not claim to have given you all the scriptural wisdom concerning the proper use of social media. I tried to make some qualifying and balancing statements along the way, but I freely acknowledge that I did not make all that could—and ultimately, should—be made. And in this case, I cannot send you a new book each week where I slowly reveal such caveats over several months. If the five questions I have presented cause pause and prayerful reflection, then my mission has been accomplished. I want to conclude with some final thoughts and perspectives concerning possible root issues that feed the misuse of social media, which I have mentioned in the previous chapters. If the following is true, then addressing these root issues could go a long way in helping us apply heavenly wisdom to this earthly tool.

Allegiance

I have already stated this, but I want to make sure I
don't leave you with the impression that it is sinful to
use social media to address or comment on political
matters or controversial news stories. Nor is it sinful
to promote the truth and righteousness contained in
God's Word. I have no desire to play lord of anyone's
conscience and lay down prohibitions where there
are none. However, even though I am not suggesting
that it is wrong to use social media in those ways, I
do not believe that Christians are obligated to do so.
Some people may believe their allegiance to Christ
requires them to use social media to expose lies,
denounce sin, and promote the gospel. They sincerely believe that this is necessary to be faithful to
Christ. Maybe that's you. You may feel it is your duty
as a believer to share a picture of an aborted fetus
with a Scripture reference—otherwise, you must be
ashamed of God's Word. Maybe you are convinced
that, as a believer, you must use social media to warn
people of the coming judgment and announce salva-
tion in Christ, or else you are ashamed of the gospel
(Rom. 1:16). Christ has clearly told us we are to confess Him before men (Matt. 10:32–33), and we are not
to be ashamed of Him or His words (Mark 8:38). We
must not cower in the fear of man, the mark of which
may sometimes be silence, when the right thing to do
is speak up for the sake of the truth (Matt. 10:26–27).
When, where, and how we do that, however, is a

matter of wisdom, not only a matter of faithfulness (Col. 4:5–6). There is no scriptural basis for believing we must use social media to expose lies, denounce sin, and promote the truth of the gospel among men. The only thing we can say with certain conviction is that we are obligated to use social media righteously so that the matter, manner, and motive please God (Ps. 19:14). To believe otherwise could, out of the fear of being unfaithful, cause some to act impulsively, not giving careful consideration to the many other biblical principles that should shape our communication.

Anonymity

Social media reminds me of the Tower of Babel— you know the story. The whole earth, as one people, determined that together they would build a city and tower that would reach the heavens. They were clear about their motivation: "Let us make a name for ourselves, lest we be scattered abroad over the face of the whole earth" (Gen. 11:4). In the context of those early chapters of Genesis, to have a name was to have attained renown or to have become famous (Gen. 6:4). Pride was at work at Babel, and it brought the judgment of God. But connected to this desire for fame was a fear of being scattered over the face of the earth. What was that about? Why did they fear that? I find myself agreeing with those who interpret it as *the fear of anonymity*. They feared that spreading out to the four corners of the earth would result in them living and dying without any substantial significance being ascribed to them. They hoped staying together would enable them to accomplish great things and cause them to never be forgotten. This great feat was to be a memorial to them for generations to come, as they would be remembered in history for their accomplishments.

How many of us struggle with the routine and monotony of everyday life in our little corner of the world? It may be an underlying fear of anonymity. We are not content to live a simple and ordinary life. We want to be *known*. We want what we are doing, thinking, and feeling to have a broader significance. Social media is like a digital Tower of Babel, in that it gives us the ability to connect globally, so we no longer feel relegated to our little corner of the world. People living in out-of-the-way locations can now share their lives with others all over the globe. You can send pictures of the deck you just built, the trip you just took, or your kid's championship trophy. Of course, there is nothing wrong with doing that in and of itself, since, as social creatures, we have a wholesome desire to share our lives with others. I wonder how much of this, though, is rooted in the fear of anonymity. The "global togetherness" of social media appears to offer us a means to make a name for ourselves. It is just a thought. Take it or leave it. But if I am right, could this be the reason why many feel compelled to share their thoughts and perspectives on social media concerning various issues and events? Could it be that they cannot bear the thought of not contributing to the conversation and being acknowledged for it? If so, this fear of anonymity could cause us to ignore the biblical principles of communication.

Affirmation

We come out of the womb with a desire for affirmation. Children look for the affirming smile of their parents. We seek affirmation from our spouses. We want the boss to tell us we are doing a good job and are an asset to the company. This desire for affirmation is not sinful. Even the encouragement Christians are to give to one another can take the form of affirmation (2 Cor. 8:7). Like every other part of our humanity, however, the desire for affirmation has been distorted by sin. Twisted by sin, our desire for affirmation can become inordinate, so that it controls us. Sadly, some people, even believers, cannot seem to live very long without receiving affirmation. Social media has definitely brought this insatiable appetite for affirmation to light. For example, someone posts on social media about how insecure he or she has always been, living for years in bondage to others' opinions and standards, always believing he or she never quite measured up. But now, finally, he or she has broken free from those chains and no longer lives in that prison. A proclamation like this is not complete without a fresh selfie of the liberated person.

This is where social media gives some great insight into human nature. Has that person truly broken free from the need for affirmation? If the person is no longer living for the approval of others, then why post such a proclamation where people will give a thumbs-up, smiley faces, or comments like "You go, girl!" "You're such an inspiration, man!" or "Cute pic. I like the new you"? If the person has truly been set free from the idol of affirmation, he or she wouldn't feel the need to be affirmed for no longer needing affirmation! This reveals that the person is still controlled by the smiles and frowns of others. If they are truly liberated, the thought of broadcasting it would probably not even cross their minds. This is just one example of how an out-of-control desire for affirmation can be a driving force in the use of social media.

Maybe you would confess that you just can't resist sharing on social media every thought, every insight, every argument, or every joke that comes to mind concerning almost every current social, political, and religious issue. If this describes you, could it be that you are being compelled by a desire for others to affirm your knowledge, wisdom, boldness, wit, and irresistible skill of communication? One possible indicator of this problem is that within minutes or seconds after you post, you are checking for responses. Like a drug addict, every time you hear the ding, you get a fresh dopamine dump, which leaves you craving for more. You are instantly troubled if certain people do not like it or leave comments. Even negative responses strangely give you a high because they might indicate that you will be featured in a future edition of Foxe's *Book of Martyrs*. If so, this inordinate desire for affirmation can cause blindness to the biblical principles of communication.

I will leave it to someone else to write a book delving more deeply into the psychological aspects of social media from a biblical perspective. But these are some concluding thoughts as to what might possibly be at the root of its misuse.

Grace: The Solution

Finally, consider briefly how the grace of God in Christ is the solution, especially to the last two roots: the fear of anonymity and the desire for affirmation. First, *grace humbles*. One aspect of humility is to recognize we are saved by grace, and all we have and are able to do is by that same grace (1 Cor. 4:6–7; 15:9–10). Grace produces a lowly perspective about ourselves (Eph. 3:8), which certainly should put a great restraint on our native tendency to do things to get attention. When we are humbly dependent on grace, we are not too concerned if others don't think of us as special (2 Cor. 12:9–10).

Second, *grace satisfies*. When the Lord called Abraham, He promised to make his name great and to make him a channel of blessing to the whole world (Gen. 12:2–3). It is not a mere coincidence that this is recorded immediately following the incident at Babel, where the people were seeking exactly that—a name. What the people at Babel were seeking by their own effort was bestowed on Abraham by grace. It could not be obtained by human effort or merit. If you are a believer in Jesus Christ, you have been blessed along with Abraham (Gal. 3:9, 23), and what you have been given by grace is substantial and eternal (Eph. 1:3). Contrast that with what the world seeks in vain and which does not last, even if it is obtained. When you understand this and truly believe it, it will satisfy your longing heart, enabling you to put to death the roots of an inordinate desire to be known and affirmed. As a dear preacher friend of mine, who is now with the Lord, once said, "My name is written in heaven. That is name and fame enough for me." Amen, my dear brother!

Third, *grace unites*. The gospel of Christ reconciles us not only to God (2 Cor. 5:18) but also to one another (Eph. 2:14–15), creating a real spiritual bond in Christ. One of the ways that spiritual bond is expressed is by Christian fellowship (Acts 2:42). I am extremely thankful for email and social media platforms, which allow me to fellowship with dear brothers and sisters in Christ who live in other places, immediately, without having to wait days or weeks for letters to arrive. As much of a blessing as that is, Scripture emphasizes the priority of fellowshipping with one another in person. When bringing one of his letters to a close, the apostle John wrote, "Having many things to write to you, I did not wish to do so with paper and ink; but I hope to come to you and speak face to face, that our joy may be full" (2 John 12). Evidently, John believed even a Spirit-inspired letter could not be an adequate substitute for in-person fellowship. You know where this is going, don't you? If a Spirit-inspired letter is not an adequate substitute for face-to-face fellowship, then certainly social media is not an adequate substitute.* We should aim at spending more time together face-to-face than we do communicating on social media. The more time we spend apart from one another, glued to our phones and computer screens, the more insensitive we will become to the biblical principles of communication. Whereas our love for one another, which is especially fostered by face-to-face fellowship, kills the roots of sinful communication, motivating us to do nothing "through selfish ambition or conceit" (Phil. 2:3) but to put one another's concerns above our own (v. 4).

May the Lord grant us all grace to tame our fingers with heavenly wisdom.

---

*This thought is based on a message my dear brother in Christ Paul Smalley preached on this text, arguing for the superiority of in-person fellowship over electronic communication.

*A special thanks to Melissa Eefsting,
who assisted me with the initial edit.
Your constant encouragement to me as your
pastor means more than you know.*